AN ASPIRING NOVELIST

essay by Jim Fergus

AN ASPIRING NOVELIST

essay by Jim Fergus

Cover designed by The Little French eBooks

Published by The Little French eBooks

Published 2024

Six or seven years ago while I was

conducting an interview with novelist Thomas McGuane, he and I were discussing some of the essential differences between writing journalism and fiction. McGuane remarked upon the fact that nearly all the journalists of his acquaintance aspired to be novelists, and he was referring to some very good writers such as Hunter Thompson and Thomas Wolfe, the latter of whom, of course, has since actually published a novel. Because interviewers frequently have to play the stooge, asking question to which they may already know the answers in order to let the subjects do the talking, I asked Tom McGuane why, if these journalists, as talented and successful as they were, really wanted to write novels so badly, didn't they? And McGuane, who as anyone who has ever held a conversation with him can attest, is more often than not right on the money, looked at me, paused a beat, then uttered the obvious: "Well, because it's so hard." Indeed.

Nearly all the journalists of my acquaintance as well harbor private aspirations to become novelists. We talk quietly, almost reverentially about the novel we intend one day to write, or about the novel we have already written, the one that resides in the bottom desk drawer or in the back of the closet, in various stages of completion. Perhaps it is complete, and our agent is trying to "place" it, but it's already made the round of a dozen or so publishing houses, and now we're thinking about re-writing it to make it more commercial, (or else just better.). As working journalists we never quite seem to have the time or the money to devote to it right now, but we mean to get to it, and the dream that we will one day make the quantum leap of both faith and talent from journalism to fiction holds at bay the nagging fear that we may end up just another journalistic John Doe--fated to the eternal anonymity of the minor leagues.   For me it's a fear as compelling in its own way as that which many single women are said to suffer of ending up bag ladies. Given the often niggardly pay scale of the writing profession many freelance journalists share that one too, though most of us have resigned ourselves to it.   I rather expect to end up a bag man, joining the growing ranks of the homeless in America, all my meagre possessions in a shopping cart, still firing off endless query letters to penurious publications which in any case often don't bother to respond.   No, if I hadn't allowed for the possibility of financial ruin from the beginning, I'd have chosen another profession; that's the least of my worries. What's really got me scared is that I won't ever get to be a novelist.

What writer hasn't dreamed of it since childhood? I can still remember the very first line of fiction I ever wrote. This was going to be a long, epic novel about a family crossing the plains in a wagon train, (In those days I was heavily influenced by Walt Disney adventures.), and the first line was a bit of dialogue spoken by the father of the clan that went: "Let's go! We got work that's got to be done. "Actually, I still think it's a pretty good line. I was only a kid.

That novel, of course, was never completed, nor was the next begun after my parents died when I was sixteen. Still a third, written when I was in my twenties did go to term, but was so resolutely bad that it had to be destroyed like a hopelessly deformed puppy. More recently I invested five years (though these were frequently interrupted by journalism assignments and the unpleasant necessity of having to earn a living), in as many drafts of a less bad, but still inadequate novel. Still I remain published only as a journalist. In the author's notes at the end of my articles I remain a "freelance writer". "Jim Fergus is a freelance writer who lives in whose work has appeared in ... ", or some variation thereof. This year an editor of a magazine to which I am an occasional contributor, knowing that I had recently completed a novel, asked if he might not say: "Jim Fergus is a freelance writer and novelist... ".

I thought it over, mightily tempted; I ached for that particular honorific. But finally I had to decline his offer. Saying so doesn't make it so, and until I had published a novel, I couldn't truly call myself a novelist. I hadn't yet earned the title. Either you break out of the minor leagues or you don't. It is that simple. But what combination of luck, talent, faith, and character gets you there, or doesn't, is not so simple.

For the journalist and aspiring novelist the process goes something like this: You chip away at your dreams, stealing a month for your novel here, two months there. In between these periods you have to go off and do something to make money, unless you are fortunate in that regard and already have some. Until before you know it a year of sporadic work has stretched away into two, then three, then four, by which time the good news is that at least everyone has finally stopped asking, "How's the Great American Novel coming along," an increasingly tiresome question, asked over the years in all its possible intonations from friendly supportive inquiry, to light teasing, to barely disguised disdain. Now mercifully they've stopped asking altogether, either mildly embarrassed for your seemingly endless labors, or else having given up faith that you are really even writing a novel. That's when they start making furtive, gentle inquiries of your wife when you aren't present. "How's the novel coming along?", the ask sympathetically, as if inquiring about the progress of a terminal disease. By this point your wife has secretly begun to entertain the frightening suspicion that maybe there isn't a novel; she recalls all too clearly the chilling scene in the film The Shining when Shelley Duval finally takes a forbidden peak at hubby Jack Nicholson's nightmarish manuscript.

I never let my wife, or anyone else, read one single page of the first four drafts of my novel, for the simple reason that I felt I hadn't got it right yet. I wanted it to be perfect, or at least as perfect as I could make it. So I asked of her, and I more or less received, a sort of blind faith, though this was neither unequivocable nor unshakable. And why should it be? My wife is a practical, thrifty, pragmatic woman, (in my opinion the best kind of wife for a writer to have as these qualities are often needed as ballast), the kind of woman who keeps a close eye on excessive paper towel consumption. About this novel writing business, she mostly kept quiet, but I knew she looked upon it with a mixture of skepticism and tolerance, much as another man's wife might tactfully ignore marital infidelity in the interest of the long haul. It was in her mind a minor, and hopefully temporary deviation on the road of life, a relatively harmless, if thoroughly unprofitable pursuit that I had to get out of my system before getting down to the real business of life--earning a living. I know this because every few months or so certain inevitable doubts bubbled to the surface, subtly phrased question posed just before we went to sleep as to my intentions of getting a "real" job after the novel was finished, just in case things didn't pan out--you know, a real job unlike freelance writing that pays real money. I might just mention that although I have over the years written for a number of well-known national publications, I have also from time to time been forced to seek alternate means of earning a living. In one such period a long time ago toward the beginning of my writing career, I was a teaching tennis pro, in another more recent, an outdoor furniture salesman. I have also, I may as well admit, borrowed heavily. None of this is unique in any way; in fact it's utterly pedestrian and seems to be the nature of the business, and I mention it only to point up the fact that my wife's doubts were by no means unjustified.

In retrospect it may have been a big mistake not to let her in on things earlier, because if you're going to demand blind faith over that length of time, then in the end you'd damn well better deliver the goods. If after five years and as many drafts you still don't get it right in the end, if you fail, then her disappointment will only be that much keener. Now it is one thing to fall short of your own dreams and expectations--they spring nearly eternal in the aspiring novelist's heart-- and quite another to shortchange the faith and patience of your wife, your friends and loved ones. For my part I could believe with each successive draft that I was winnowing, honing, perfecting, coming that much closer to the truth I sought, which is after all the quest of fiction. It is also the beauty and the grace of the writing process itself, that which allows you, not just to go on, but to do so eagerly, with confidence in your skills and faith in the final product. "The only thing that keeps you going through the shit years," the poet-novelist Jim Harrison once said to me, "is your own conception of yourself."

And therein lies the danger too, for these same illusions that keep you going can also destroy you. There comes a time when you must put down the pen, declare once and for all that this is finished, as good as you can make it, and then face the gaping disparity between your intentions and your skills, the truth that you have still not got it right, and are perhaps incapable of doing so. So that what kept you afloat all those years through all those successive drafts, (not that you didn't have moments of self-doubt and even despair), the belief that you were honing and improving, may have been nothing more than a desperate losing fight against your own limitations as a writer. The final vindication for your time and labors was to have been this finished product, and now here it is for all to see, but looking more like some kind of unidentiable scat, than the sleek living thing you had imagined. Then you pay the fiddler for the music to which you have danced for the past five years, or however long it has been, your currency that same old nagging fear that you are indeed still John Doe the freelance writer, still the aspiring novelist, not the real novelist that you had for a brief and brilliant moment quite fervently believed. Your carriage has turned back into a pumpkin.

My worst suspicions were confirmed as initial reactions to my novel trickled in. Upon finally reading it my wife adopted an inscrutable, neutral position. Diplomatically she allowed as how she liked some parts of it, didn't like others, and that she was really too close to it to be able to offer an objective opinion. I had clearly not wowed her as I had so badly hoped to do, which was to have been the payoff for her patience. I called that strike one. Then the agent to whom I sent the novel responded. A successful, highly regarded agent who handles some very fine novelists, he is a no-bullshit, bottom-line kind of guy for whom I have great respect, and he delivered his pronouncement with the same precise, brutal efficiency as the sledgehammer coup de grace that used to be administered to cattle at the slaughterhouse. "I don't think I can sell this book," he said simply. Strike two, and I never even saw the pitch. The third person to report back on my novel was a brilliant young editor, the daughter of a great novelist of my acquaintance, and a woman of impeccable literary instincts of her own But why go on? Even recalling this time still brings a flush of shame and failure to my face. Suffice it to say that I went down swinging.

Let's recap what's taken place here in the aspiring novelist's life: You have disappointed your faithful wife, and as word gets out, your friends and loved ones--all those who wished you well, who believed in you. It is a very public business. Almost as bad it might be added, you've satisfied those few enemies who wished to see you fail. Barely worth mentioning, you've broken your own heart to boot. It is as if you've suddenly woken up and discovered that you have actually reproduced almost word for word that horrifying manuscript from The Shining, and now you look upon it with equal parts disgust and wonder that anyone on earth could work so long and so hard and produce something so lifeless, so utterly loathsome. You look around for a large rock to crawl under, leaving behind nothing but your trail of slime.

Of course, it's probably not as bad as all that, though it may as well be, for there are no gradations in the aspiring novelist's mind between good and bad; it is either one or the other. Mine was clearly the latter. Meanwhile, there was the concurrent matter of having spun my wheels for five years, and suddenly finding myself--surprise!--exactly that many years older. During this time I had watched the meteoric rise of a number of very young, very precocious novelists--some quite good, some rather mediocre, some frankly not so good--and as I plodded away at my own work, far too old to worry about precocity, I tried hard not to begrudge any of them their good fortune. I had also watched as friends with more normal, stable jobs, who earlier in the decade had been pretty much in the same financial boat as I, began to come into their own, buying new houses and cars and other trappings which seem to signal successful adulthood in America. One such friend failed at his own small business, went through a training program and got a job with a major brokerage house, began pulling down a couple hundred g's a year, bought a new house, and a new car that was more expensive than my house--all in the period in which I pecked away at the same preposterous novel, driving the same old beater car. Such advancements in the material world were not lost on my wife, who I suspect secretly began to wish she had married more of an L.A. Law kind of guy.

Now there you are, the aspiring novelist, instantly five years older, as in some variation of the Dorian Gray theme, having given the tail end of your youth to your novel, a bad novel, it must be said, with the frightful sense that you are at a dead standstill without having gotten out of the starting gate. That well-documented feeling of disquiet, the inchoate urgency of impending middle age known as the mid-life crisis is really nothing more than the first clear glimpse of mortality, and with the handwriting thus on the wall, it is for many novelists, who recognize that there are a finite number of years left in which to write a finite number of books, a time of increased effort and increased output. However, when you come into this age with a fresh failure under your belt, you're all dressed up with nowhere to go.

The hot flash of shame and searing disappointment that you felt initially, gives way rather quickly to a relatively benign numbness, a sort of stupefaction. You do a lot of brooding, mulling things over. Perhaps you drink a bit more than usual or a lot. Perhaps you start smoking again, something which you gave up several years ago. In the worst possible case scenario you have a complete nervous collapse and have to be hospitalized, or even worse than that you blow your brains out with both barrels of a .12-gauge shotgun. Having given the latter alternative some consideration, and hopefully, having rejected it, what you're wondering now is what exactly your next move is going to be. All along you had been very careful not to have unrealistic expectations for your novel. You had avoided, for instance, excessive fantasizing about seeing your picture on the front page of The New York Times Book Review. Still, in spite of your wife's practical prodding, you had made no real contingent plans.

The numbness deepens to a kind of total paralysis, through which occasional glitches of terrifying clarity begin to surge. Recognizing that only work can get you back on track, you quickly fire off twelve or fifteen query letters along with clips of your work to various magazine editors. Naturally, you also need to make some money. You spend the next month and a half checking the mailbox, in which time maybe one or two of the editors respond, (It is axiomatic that editors are much busier than writers.), now and the glitches, increased in strength and frequency, have entered your dream life, jolting you awake in the middle of the night, at that stone quiet surreal hour when you are most defenseless; you come awake as if zapped by a cattle prod, sweating and terror-stricken with the realization that you have no prospects, not one. Unable to go back to sleep, for the remainder of the night insane plans for brand new careers are hatched in the sense- less waking dreams of insomnia. In one such dream of mine I got a job as a piano player at a piano bar. It was a good job. I got free cocktails and happy, well-dressed patrons stuffed dollar bills and sometimes even fives and tens into a giant cognac glass on top of the piano while I played and sang their favorites. It was dawn before it occurred to me that not only can't I play the piano, I can't even hold a tune.

That's when I decided to burn all copies of my novel, all five drafts. This seemed a radical solution, and a distressing one to contemplate, but I began to see it as a necessity, in the same way that the Forest Service must periodically execute controlled burns of timber in order to prevent more cataclysmic conflagrations and to allow for future regrowth. I hadn't quite screwed up the courage to do it yet, because, loathsome though they may be, they were nevertheless the only tangible thing I had to show for those five years of my life.

Then as the fifth and final draft sat there on my desk, neatly spiral bound in mimicry of a real book, a strange process began. I began to hear faint, plaintive murmurs issuing from it. In the ensuing days the murmurs began to take shape, to become better defined, louder, more insistent, until I could no longer ignore them. They were the voices of some of my characters, crying out for my attention. One demanded to be more fully realized, another to be less of a caricature. A third, a protagonist, a hermit and stoic of sorts, begged for more texture in his life. An interesting idea that--more texture in a hermit's life. Three or four minor characters actually asked to be released from the novel altogether: "A mistake has been made," they protested, "We don't belong here." What began as a few dislocated and unintelligible cries soon escalated into a general uproar, a full-fledged riot. I hardly dared open the book for fear that I would be dragged inside and held hostage. I could still burn it, quelling the riot and silencing these characters forever. Or I could hear them out, listen to their grievances, negotiate. That seemed the only sensible course of action.

Hope raises her weary head once again to the aspiring novelist, saves you time and time again. Just when things seem darkest you recall the grace of youthful dreams, and from across the years but still somehow from within the pages of your novel you hear yet another voice, the pure clear voice of a child, a familiar voice, your own, uniquely yours. Mine says: "Let's go. We got work that's got to be done."